Microsoft Excel for Beginner: Book 2

RIYANTO, ARIS
&
MARLIANITA, RINI

ISBN:
- (ebook)
9798860498013 (paperback)
9798860498440 (hardcover)

GGKEY:
-

Author:
Aris Riyanto
Rini Marlianita

Reviewer:
Tim dosen Politeknik LP3I

Cover:
-

DEDICATION

I dedicate this book to my children
(I.N. Arundaya & I.A. Karim), wife, and all students
around the world, especially students from the LP3I
Polytechnic.

FOREWORD

We would like to express our gratitude to Allah SWT for His guidance and support in completing the book titled "Microsoft Excel for Beginners: Book 2." This book is a continuation of Book 1, which provides a practical 14-day guide to mastering Excel for those who are embarking on their journey into the world of Microsoft Excel, a powerful tool that has aided millions of people worldwide in managing data, analysing information, and creating informative reports.

In this increasingly digital world, Excel skills are becoming crucial in various aspects of life, including business, education, and daily activities. This book is specifically designed to help beginners understand and master the fundamentals of Excel, from basic calculations to creating compelling charts.

We have compiled this book using simple language and a practical approach. Your journey begins with understanding the Excel interface and the basic steps to create, save, and open files. Subsequently, you will delve deeper into learning essential functions, formulas, and calculations that are valuable in your daily work.

Throughout this journey, you will encounter real-life examples that allow you to apply the knowledge you have acquired. All of this is aimed at enabling you to experience the immediate benefits of using Excel in your everyday activities. We extend our heartfelt thanks to the entire writing team who worked diligently to create the content of this book. We also appreciate the readers who have provided us with support and inspiration.

We hope that this book will be of great benefit to you. Happy reading, and best of luck in embarking on your new journey to master Microsoft Excel!

Warm regards,
Aris Riyanto & Rini Marlianita
September 2023

CONTENTS

8 PREPARATIONS

Introduction

Microsoft Excel is one of the electronic spreadsheet application programs developed by Microsoft. A spreadsheet application is used to organize, analyse, and store data in a tabular format. Excel is a part of the Microsoft Office suite of applications, which also includes Word, PowerPoint, and others.

The primary function of Microsoft Excel is to enable users to create, edit, and save data in the form of cells within a worksheet. Each cell can contain text, numbers, mathematical formulas, or other functions. These cells can be arranged in rows and columns to form a table or worksheet.

Excel offers various features that allow users to perform various tasks, such as:

1. Calculating and analysing data: Excel provides

various mathematical and statistical functions that can be used to calculate and analyse data, including arithmetic operations, mathematical formulas, and statistical functions.

2. Creating charts and diagrams: Excel allows users to create charts and diagrams based on data within the worksheet. These graphics help present data in a visually understandable manner.

3. Sorting data: Users can organize data in tables, sort data based on specific criteria, filter data to display only entries that meet certain criteria, and more.

4. Formatting: Excel allows users to format cells, rows, columns, and the entire worksheet in various ways, including changing text styles, adding colours, or applying specific rules.

5. Creating formulas and functions: Excel has an internal programming language that allows users to create custom formulas and functions that enable automation of calculations based on specific data.

Microsoft Excel is widely used in various fields, including business, academia, finance, project management, data analysis, and more. With its broad utility and powerful features, Excel has become an essential tool for managing data and daily tasks in many organizations and companies.

Preparations

To operate Microsoft Excel, you will need:

Option 1 (Online):
1. A laptop or desktop computer.
2. A web browser.
3. Internet connection.
4. A Microsoft account.

Option 2 (Offline):
1. A laptop or desktop computer.
2. Microsoft Excel application installed.

Option 1 is an online option where learners are not required to install the Excel application but need a stable internet connection. Option 2 is an offline option where learners are required to install the Excel application on their own devices.

How to use

Open the Microsoft excel application, the first way is to press the start button, open a browser application (e.g., Google Chrome) then open www.office.com then log in using a Microsoft account.

Office is now Microsoft 365

The all-new Microsoft 365 lets you create, share and collaborate all in one place with your favourite apps

| Sign in | Get Microsoft 365 |

Sign up for the free version of Microsoft 365 >

If using the offline option, then the steps are as follows. Open the Microsoft excel application by pressing the start button, type "excel" press enter, so that the excel application opens as shown in the picture.

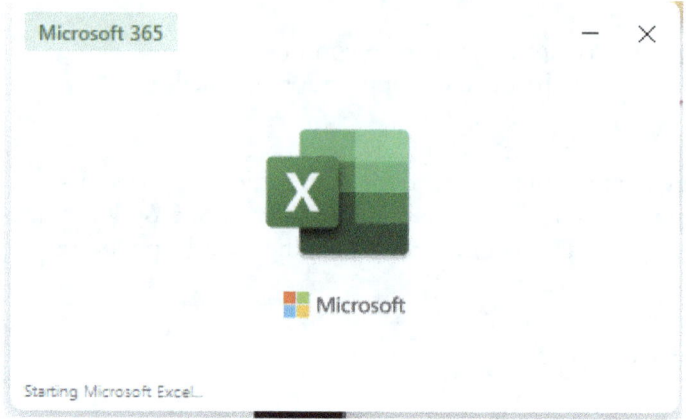

When the Microsoft Excel application is open, a worksheet called "worksheet" will open, with sheet1 or sheet1 as the main sheet. (See image below)

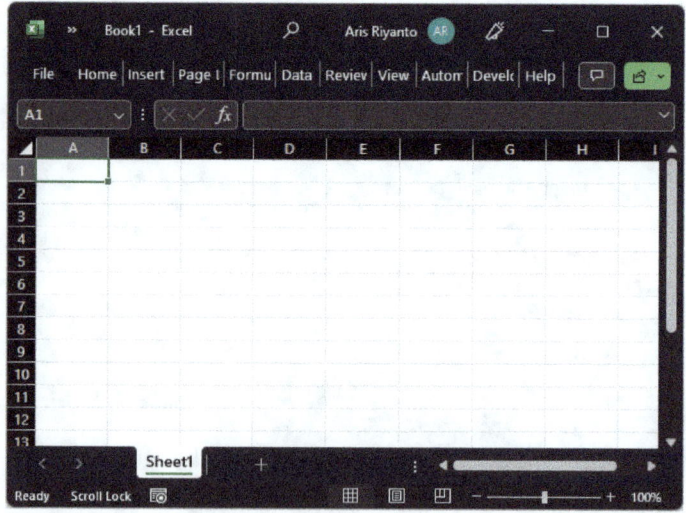

At the top there are several menus known as "ribbon bars" where these menus are not much different from the menus in other office applications, for example Microsoft

Word. Therefore, if students already use other office applications, then to operate Excel will be more familiar. At the top there are several menus known as "ribbon bars" where these menus are not much different from the menus in other office applications, for example Microsoft Word. Therefore, if students already use other office applications, then to operate Excel will be more familiar.

Then underneath there is A1 and fx.
- A1 represents the currently selected cell, whereas.
- Fx is a place to enter data, commands, or formulas.

Underneath there are horizontal boxes A B C D E etc. and vertical boxes on the left side numbered 1-2-3 etc.

- A B C etc. is also called a column, so if you say it is called column A, then what is meant is the position from box A to the bottom. Likewise, column B C and so on
- 1-2-3 and so on are also called rows or rows. So, for example it is called the 1st row, so what is meant is the position from the 1st box to the right side so on. So did the 2nd row and others.
  - Cell is a meeting between columns and rows. Then A1 is the selected cell, which means it is the meeting between the 1st row and column A.

Towards the lowermost section (as depicted in the image above), you will observe "Sheet1" accompanied by a "+" symbol.

- Sheet1 is the available worksheet. It can also be said as a page in Excel.
- The "+" sign is a button to add the next sheet if needed. Which when pressed it will appear

"sheet2" and so on.

How to use 2

Excel serves as a proficient number processor where users can generate and input data in the format of columns and rows. This feature makes Excel highly suitable for storing data in the form of tables, which can be subjected to various calculation and processing operations.

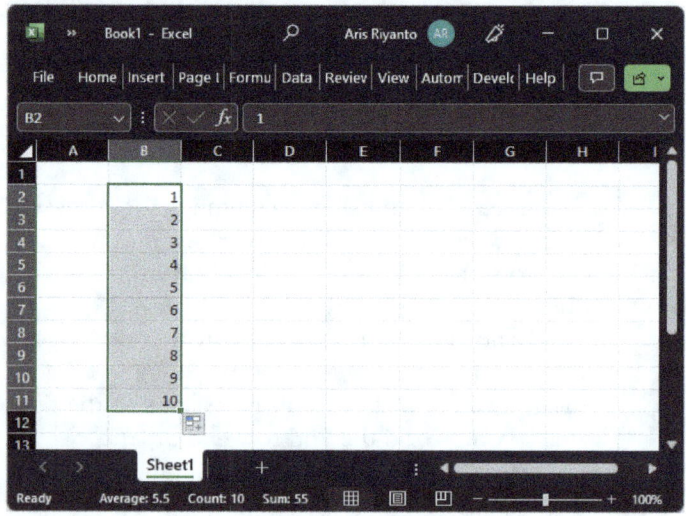

To create a series of numbers from 1 to 10 in Excel, you can use the Fill Handle feature or use the "Series" option from the "Fill" menu. Here are two methods to achieve this:

Method 1: Using the Fill Handle
1. Type "1" in cell B2.
2. Move your cursor to the bottom-right corner of cell B2 until it changes to a plus sign (+) called the Fill Handle.

3.   Click and drag the Fill Handle down to cell B11.
     Excel will automatically fill the cells with the series
     of numbers from 1 to 10.

Method 2: Using the "Series" Option
1.   Type "1" in cell B2.
2.   Type "10" in cell B3 (the last number of the
     series).
3.   Select both cells B2 and B3.
4.   Go to the "Home" tab on the Excel ribbon.
5.   In the "Editing" group, click on "Fill," and then
     select "Series..."
6.   In the "Series" dialog box, choose "Columns" for
     "Series in," and "Linear" for "Type."
7.   Set the "Step Value" to 1 (since you want a series
     from 1 to 10).
8.   Click "OK," and Excel will create the series of
     numbers from 1 to 10 in cells B2 to B11.

Both methods will give you the same result, a series of
numbers from 1 to 10 in column B of your Excel
worksheet.

9 MULTIPLE IF

As discussed in the previous book, in spreadsheet applications, we can solve logical problems using the IF logical function. For example, determining whether a student has passed or failed an exam can be calculated using the IF formula.

However, sometimes the criteria needed are more than just two; they could be three, four, or even more. In cases like this, there will be multiple IF functions to address the issue. To simplify the expression of these multiple conditions, we refer to it as the "MULTIPLE IF" formula.

Example scenario:

The scenario is when we determine the grade or numeric value for school or college exam results. For instance, if the score is equal to or above 90, the grade is "Excellent," if it's equal to or above 80, the grade is "Good," and so on. For a more detailed breakdown, please refer to the table below.

Point >=	Predicate	Grade
90	Very well	A
80	Good	B
70	Enough	C
60	Not enough	D
0	Bad	E

Let's position and configure our Excel application as shown in the image below:

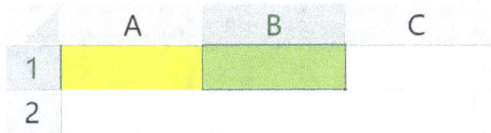

Explanation:
1. The yellow cell (A1) is the input cell where values will be entered.
2. The green cell (B1) is the result cell where the formula will be entered.

Enter the following formula in B1:

=IF(A1>=90, "A", IF(A1>=80, "B", IF(A1>=70, "C", IF(A1>=60, "D", "E"))))

Then it will produce results like this.:

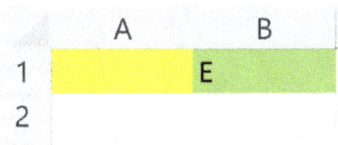

We enter the exam result value in cell A1, let's assume the score is 78. Then cell B1 will change according to the conditions in the table above.

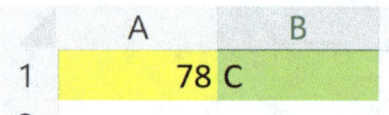

Please create the following table and then apply the rules and formulas that have been learned:

	A	B	C	D	E
1	No.	NAME	POINT	PREDICATE	GRADE
2		1 JOHN	51		
3		2 SMITH	83		
4		3 FATIMA	77		
5		4 ALI	56		
6		5 OMAR	93		

To work with cell E2, the initial formula needs to be modified and adjusted. It should change from this:

`=IF(A1>=90, "A", IF(A1>=80, "B", IF(A1>=70, "C", IF(A1>=60,"D", "E"))))`

To:

`=IF(C2>=90, "A", IF(C2>=80, "B", IF(C2>=70, "C", IF(C2>=60,"D", "E"))))`

Place this formula in cell E2, and you will get results like this.

	A	B	C	D	E
1	No.	NAME	POINT	PREDICATE	GRADE
2	1 JOHN		51		E
3	2 SMITH		83		
4	3 FATIMA		77		
5	4 ALI		56		

For the cells below it, simply copy cell E2 and paste it into cells E3 to E6 without the need to type the formulas one by one.

In cell E3:

`` `=IF(E3>=90, "Very well", IF(E3>=80, "Good", IF(E3>=70, "Enough", IF(E3>=60, "Not enough", "Bad"))))` ``

In cell E4:

`` `=IF(E4>=90, "Very well", IF(E4>=80, "Good", IF(E4>=70, "Enough", IF(E4>=60, "Not enough", "Bad"))))` ``

In cell E5:

`` `=IF(E5>=90, "Very well", IF(E5>=80, "Good", IF(E5>=70, "Enough", IF(E5>=60, "Not enough", "Bad"))))` ``

In cell E6:

`` `=IF(E6>=90, "Very well", IF(E6>=80, "Good", IF(E6>=70, "Enough", IF(E6>=60, "Not enough", "Bad"))))` ``

Remember, there's no need to manually type the above formulas. Simply copy and paste, or double-click on cell E2, and each formula above will calculate the same criteria for the respective cells (E2, E3, E4, E5, E6) based on the values in each of those cells with relevant adjustments. You can copy this formula to the appropriate cells as needed without typing it out one by one.

This will result in a table like this:

	A	B	C	D	E
1	No.	NAME	POINT	PREDICATE	GRADE
2		1 JOHN	51		E
3		2 SMITH	83		B
4		3 FATIMA	77		C
5		4 ALI	56		E
6		5 OMAR	93		A

How about the PREDICATE? We can enter this formula in cell D2 referring to the previous condition table:

`=IF(C2>=90, "Very well", IF(C2>=80, "Good", IF(C2>=70, "Enough", IF(C2>=60, "Not enough", "Bad"))))`

This will result in the following table:

	A	B	C	D	E
1	No.	NAME	POINT	PREDICATE	GRADE
2		1 JOHN	51	Bad	E
3		2 SMITH	83		B
4		3 FATIMA	77		C
5		4 ALI	56		E
6		5 OMAR	93		A

As a practice exercise and to sharpen your skills, please complete the empty cells according to the explanations and discussions mentioned earlier.

This will result in a complete table like this:

	A	B	C	D	E
1	No.	NAME	POINT	PREDICATE	GRADE
2	1	JOHN	51	Bad	E
3	2	SMITH	83	Good	B
4	3	FATIMA	77	Enough	C
5	4	ALI	56	Bad	E
6	5	OMAR	93	Very well	A

A complete and comprehensive table, with the addition of borders to each cell, would look like table above.

10 LOOKUP FUNCTION

In addition to using the IF function to solve logic problems with multiple possible answers, in some cases, it is easier and quicker to use the LOOKUP function. In the example of section 9, there's a case where we want to find the PREDICATE and GRADE values, which were initially solved using the IF function. However, using the IF function is not very efficient and not recommended when there are more than three possible answers.

If there are only three possible answers, like A, B, & C, then the IF function can be used. But when there are more possibilities, like in the previous example with A, B, C, D, & E, using IF becomes prone to errors due to long and complex formulas. It's easy to make typos or forget to include commas or quotation marks within such formulas.

The solution to this issue, as I recommend, is to use LOOKUP functions available in spreadsheet applications.

Let's revisit the condition table mentioned earlier:

Value >=	Predicate	Grade
90	Very well	A
80	Good	B
70	Enough	C
60	Not enough	D
0	Bad	E

Let's recreate the value table:

No.	NAME	POINT	PREDICATE	GRADE
1	JOHN	51		
2	SMITH	83		
3	FATIMA	77		
4	ALI	56		
5	OMAR	93		

Before discussing various LOOKUP functions, let's first solve this case using the LOOKUP function as an alternative to the IF function.

First, we create a value table in the spreadsheet application as follows:

	A	B	C	D	E
1	No.	NAME	POINT	PREDICATE	GRADE
2		1 JOHN	51		
3		2 SMITH	83		
4		3 FATIMA	77		
5		4 ALI	56		
6		5 OMAR	93		

Note: The position can be adjusted according to your preference, but I recommend creating the table in the same position as shown in the example to avoid confusion.

Next, we need to copy the condition table into the same document, although it's possible to place it in a different document. However, doing so in the same document will make the process smoother without any issues.

For example, we create the condition table right next to the value table or the main table. See the image below:

	A	B	C	D	E	F	G	H	I
1	No.	NAME	POINT	PREDICATE	GRADE		Nilai >=	Predikat	Grade
2	1	JOHN	51				90	Very well	A
3	2	SMITH	83				80	Good	B
4	3	FATIMA	77				70	Enough	C
5	4	ALI	56				60	Not enough	D
6	5	OMAR	93				0	Bad	E

From the image above, you can see that the condition table starts in cell G1. You can actually place this table anywhere you want.

The next step is to sort the condition table from the smallest value to the largest value. Initially, the value 90 was at the top, but we sort it to be at the bottom, making 0 the top value.

Point >=	Predicate	Grade
0	Bad	E
60	Not enough	D
70	Enough	C

16

80	Good	B
90	Very well	A

To sort the table, right-click on the "Value >=" cell, then select "Sort Smallest to Largest."

The table above is the sorted table.

Let's first solve the PREDICATE in cell D2 using the following formula:

`=VLOOKUP(C2,$G:$I,2,TRUE)`

This will result in values as shown in the table below:

	A	B	C	D	E
1	No.	NAME	POINT	PREDICATE	GRADE
2	1	JOHN	51	Bad	
3	2	SMITH	83		
4	3	FATIMA	77		
5	4	ALI	56		
6	5	OMAR	93		

Now, let's do the same to solve the GRADE in cell E2 using the following formula:

`=VLOOKUP(C2,$G:$I,3,TRUE)`

This will result in values as shown in the table below:

	A	B	C	D	E
1	No.	NAME	POINT	PREDICATE	GRADE
2	1	JOHN	51	Bad	E
3	2	SMITH	83		
4	3	FATIMA	77		
5	4	ALI	56		
6	5	OMAR	93		

Remember, there's no need to manually type the formulas to fill in the empty cells below. Simply copy and paste or double-click on cells D2 & E2, and each formula will calculate the same criteria for the respective cells (E2, E3, E4, E5, E6) based on the values in each of those cells with relevant adjustments. You can copy this formula to the appropriate cells as needed without typing it out one by one.

Types of LOOKUP Functions:

There are several types of LOOKUP functions that can be used to solve specific cases, including:

1. LOOKUP: The LOOKUP function can be used to find a value in a single column or row and return the corresponding value from a different column or row. Microsoft itself does not recommend this function and suggests using more specific functions like HLOOKUP or VLOOKUP.

2. HLOOKUP (Horizontal Lookup): Like VLOOKUP, HLOOKUP is used to search for a value in a horizontal row and return a matching value from the same row in a different column.

3. VLOOKUP (Vertical Lookup): This function is used to search for a value in a vertical column and return a matching value from the same row in a different column.

4. XLOOKUP: XLOOKUP is a more powerful and flexible version of VLOOKUP and HLOOKUP, allowing you to search for data based on multiple criteria and return the matching result. XLOOKUP is a relatively newer function and may not be fully compatible with older spreadsheet applications. Currently, it is supported in Google Sheets and Excel 365 or Excel Online.

There are other functions that can be used as alternatives to lookup functions, such as CHOOSE and MATCH. However, in this chapter, we will focus on the four functions mentioned above.

LOOKUP

The LOOKUP function is often used to find a value within a range of data and return the corresponding value from a different range, such as looking up the name or code of a product to find its price or additional information.

Consider using VLOOKUP, as it is considered more modern and is seen as an improved replacement for LOOKUP.

However, if you'd like to learn about LOOKUP, here's an example of how to use it in a spreadsheet:

Let's say we have two data tables containing a list of products and their prices, like this:

	A	B	C	D	E
1	PRODUCT	CATEGORY		CATEGORY	PRICE
2	PRODUCT A	CAT 1		CAT 1	$ 8.00
3	PRODUCT B	CAT 2		CAT 2	$ 4.00
4	PRODUCT C	CAT 3		CAT 3	$11.00
5	PRODUCT D	CAT 4		CAT 4	$ 5.00
6	PRODUCT E	CAT 5		CAT 5	$ 6.00
7	PRODUCT F	CAT 6		CAT 6	$12.00

Let's call the above tables the "Product Table" and the "Price Table." Then we create another table in a different part of the worksheet, like this:

	G	H	I	J
1	No.	PRODUCT	CATEGORY	PRICE
2	1	PRODUCT C		
3	2			
4	3			
5	4			
6	5			
7				

Explanation:
1. Column H, highlighted in yellow, is a placeholder where we will type the product names, such as "PRODUCT C" (as in cell H2) or other product names from the Product Table.
2. Column I, highlighted in green, is the column where we will practice the LOOKUP formula to find information such as the category of the product, we input in column H.
3. Column J, highlighted in pink, is the column where we will practice the LOOKUP formula to find information about the price of the product, we input in column H.

The formula we write in cell I2 is:

`=LOOKUP(H2,A:A,B:B)`

This will result in the value "CAT 3" as shown in the image below, according to the conditions in the condition table.

No.	PRODUCT	CATEGORY	PRICE
1	PRODUCT C	CAT 3	
2			
3			
4			
5			

Do the same to solve the PRICE column using the LOOKUP formula. However, to work on the PRICE, the formula used in CATEGORY must be adjusted first.

Initial formula:

`=LOOKUP(H2,A:A,B:B)`

Changed to:

`=LOOKUP(H2,A:A,E:E)`

Assuming that the Product Table and Price Table are in the same position as shown here. Alternatively, you can use this formula:

`=LOOKUP(I2, D:D,E:E)`

In the above formula and the previous formula, it will result in the same values as shown in the table below:

No.	PRODUCT	CATEGORY	PRICE
1	PRODUCT C	CAT 3	11
2			
3			
4			
5			

You can manually enter the product names in the PRODUCT column, but there's no need to manually enter data in the CATEGORY and PRICE columns one by one. You can simply copy-paste or use the fill handle technique.

Remember, there's no need to manually type the rest of formulas. Simply copy and paste, or double-click on cell I2 and J2, and each formula above will calculate the same criteria for the respective cells (J2, J3, J4, J5, J6) based on the values in each of those cells with relevant adjustments. You can copy this formula to the appropriate cells as needed without typing it out one by one.

From the above example, it can be concluded that:
The LOOKUP formula is used to find a value within a range of data and return the corresponding value from a different range. Here is the general structure of the LOOKUP formula:

`=LOOKUP(lookup_value,                lookup_vector, result_vector)`

Here, the components are as follows:

1. `lookup_value`: This is the value you want to search for in the `lookup_vector`. The LOOKUP function will attempt to match this value with values in the `lookup_vector`.

2. `lookup_vector`: This is the range of data containing the values to be matched with the `lookup_value`. The LOOKUP function will search for the `lookup_value` within the `lookup_vector`.

3. `result_vector`: This is the range of data containing the values that correspond to the `lookup_value`. The LOOKUP function will return the value from the `result_vector` that is in the same position as the matched value in the `lookup_vector`.

The LOOKUP function will try to find a value that matches the `lookup_value` in the `lookup_vector` and then return the corresponding value from the `result_vector`. However, it's important to note that the LOOKUP function will only work if the values in the `lookup_vector` are sorted in ascending order, and if a match is not found, it will return the nearest smaller value from the `lookup_value`.

Additionally, it's worth mentioning that in many cases, using the INDEX MATCH or VLOOKUP functions, or even the newer XLOOKUP function, is often recommended over using the LOOKUP function because they provide more flexibility and control over searching and returning values.

VLOOKUP

The VLOOKUP function is an alternative to LOOKUP and is considered better and more flexible.

Before discussing VLOOKUP, let's solve the previous example using LOOKUP, and then we'll modify and solve it using the VLOOKUP function to understand the differences between the two.

Let's recreate the tables as discussed earlier:

	A	B	C	D	E
1	PRODUCT	CATEGORY		CATEGORY	PRICE
2	PRODUCT A	CAT 1		CAT 1	$ 8.00
3	PRODUCT B	CAT 2		CAT 2	$ 4.00
4	PRODUCT C	CAT 3		CAT 3	$11.00
5	PRODUCT D	CAT 4		CAT 4	$ 5.00
6	PRODUCT E	CAT 5		CAT 5	$ 6.00
7	PRODUCT F	CAT 6		CAT 6	$12.00

Let's create the next table:

	G	H	I	J
1	No.	PRODUCT	CATEGORY	PRICE
2	1	PRODUCT C		
3	2			
4	3			
5	4			
6	5			
7				

To solve the CATEGORY and PRICE columns using VLOOKUP, use the following formulas:

In cell I2:

`` `=VLOOKUP(H2,A:B,2,1)` ``

This will result in the same value, "CAT 3," as shown in the previous example.

G	H	I	J
No.	PRODUCT	CATEGORY	PRICE
1	PRODUCT C	CAT 3	
2			
3			
4			
5			

For the PRICE column, you can use this formula in cell J2:

`=VLOOKUP(I2,D:E,2,1)`

This will result in the value "11," as shown in the previous example.

G	H	I	J
No.	PRODUCT	CATEGORY	PRICE
1	PRODUCT C	CAT 3	11
2			
3			
4			
5			

You can manually enter the product names in the PRODUCT column, but there's no need to manually enter data in the CATEGORY and PRICE columns one by one. You can simply copy-paste or use the fill handle technique.

Remember, there's no need to manually type the rest of formulas. Simply copy and paste, or double-click on cell I2 and J2, and each formula above will calculate the same criteria for the respective cells (J2, J3, J4, J5, J6) based on the values in each of those cells with relevant adjustments. You can copy this formula to the appropriate cells as

25

needed without typing it out one by one.

Now, let's try another case study. We will attempt to solve the case study from the previous exercise, which involved determining predicates and grades, as previously done using multiple IF statements.

To try this formula, let's revisit the case study discussed in the multiple IF section.

Let's recreate the table as discussed in the MULTIPLE IF section:

	A	B	C	D	E
1	Point >=	Predicate	Grade		
2	90	Very well	A		
3	80	Good	B		
4	70	Enough	C		
5	60	Not enough	D		
6	0	Bad	E		

We'll call the table above the "criteria table."

However, to be used as a reference table with VLOOKUP, the data in the first column must be sorted from smallest to largest. To sort the data, right-click the cell containing "Point >=" and select "Sort," then choose "A to Z," as shown below:

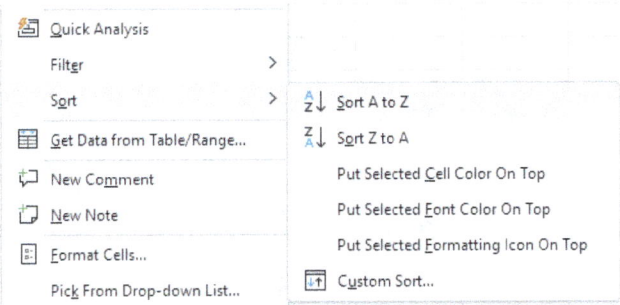

The table appearance after sorting the data will look like this:

	A	B	C	D	E
1	Point >=	Predicate	Grade		
2	0	Bad	E		
3	60	Not enough	D		
4	70	Enough	C		
5	80	Good	B		
6	90	Very well	A		
7					

Next, let's recreate the main table or simply clear the main table used in the previous exercise, so it looks like this:

	A	B	C	D	E	F
1	NO.	NAME	POINT	PREDICATE	GRADE	
2	1	JOHN	51			
3	2	SMITH	83			
4	3	FATIMA	77			
5	4	ALI	56			
6	5	OMAR	93			
7						

From the previous table, which was worked on using multiple IF statements, we will now attempt to solve it using VLOOKUP.

To complete the PREDICATE, enter the following formula in cell D2:

`=VLOOKUP(C2,Sheet1!A:C,2,1)`

Compare this to the formula you would need to enter if using the IF function:

`=IF(C2>=90, "Very well", IF(C2>=80, "Good", IF(C2>=70, "Enough", IF(C2>=60, "Not enough", "Bad")))`

Note: Sheet1 is the name of the sheet where the criteria table is located; the appearance may vary depending on where you create the criteria table.

Do the same for cell E2; enter the following formula:

`=VLOOKUP(D2,Sheet1!B:D,2,1)`

Note: You can type the formula manually or copy and paste it from cell D2 to cell E2 or drag the formula from D2 to E2.

For the cells below, there's no need to type the formula one by one; simply copy the formula from the cell above and paste it into the cells below.

This will result in values as shown in the table below:

	A	B	C	D	E
1	No.	NAME	POINT	PREDICATE	GRADE
2	1	JOHN	51	Bad	E
3	2	SMITH	83	Good	B
4	3	FATIMA	77	Enough	C
5	4	ALI	56	Bad	E
6	5	OMAR	93	Very well	A

According to the author, it is much easier to solve this case using VLOOKUP compared to IF, because the IF function has a more complex and lengthy syntax, while VLOOKUP is very simple; you just need to create a reference table for the values to be used as a lookup.

Here's a brief explanation of the VLOOKUP function. The VLOOKUP (Vertical Lookup) formula has the following structure:

`=VLOOKUP(lookup_value, table_array, col_index_num, [range_lookup])`

Below is a brief explanation of each argument in the VLOOKUP formula:

1. `lookup_value`: This is the value you want to find in the first column of the data range (`table_array`). For example, if you want to find a product's name, this would be the product name you're searching for.

2. `table_array`: This is the data range that contains the values you want to search for and the values you want to return. This range must include the column where you're searching for values (the first

column is the search column) and the column where you want to return matching values. This range can be a range of cells, a table, or a named range.

3. `col_index_num`: This is the column number within the data range (`table_array`) where the value you want to return is located. For example, if the value you want to return is in the second column of the data range, you would specify the number 2.

4. `[range_lookup]` (Optional): This is an optional argument. If you want an exact match (the value must match exactly), use `FALSE` or `0`. If you want to find the nearest match (a value that approximately matches if an exact match is not found), use `TRUE` or `1`. If you omit this argument, Excel will assume `TRUE` by default.

The VLOOKUP formula allows you to search for a value in the first column of the `table_array`, then return a corresponding value from the specified column within the same table. In practice, you would replace the values and data ranges as needed to search for and retrieve data in your spreadsheet.

HLOOKUP

HLOOKUP is a variant of the VLOOKUP function. While VLOOKUP performs a vertical lookup, HLOOKUP performs a horizontal or row-based lookup.

To practice this formula, we can't use the same example as with LOOKUP and VLOOKUP because HLOOKUP requires the table to be arranged horizontally, whereas tables in LOOKUP, VLOOKUP, and most other cases are created vertically. However, if you've mastered and understand how to use the VLOOKUP function, you won't encounter significant difficulties in applying the HLOOKUP formula.

Let's go ahead and practice the HLOOKUP formula with a different example.

Suppose we have the following data table containing information about students and their test scores:

	A	B	C	D	E	F	G
1		TEST 01	TEST 02	TEST 03	TEST 04	TEST 05	
2	STUDENT 01	32	79	19	85	86	
3	STUDENT 02	62	45	10	95	71	
4	STUDENT 03	21	75	24	39	77	
5	STUDENT 04	57	48	84	57	57	
6	STUDENT 05	75	63	51	58	20	
7							

In this example, we want to find a student's test score using the HLOOKUP function.

Here are the steps:

1. Create a new table where we will enter the test name, and the test score will automatically appear based on the selected student's name.

2. In the table below, type the test name in cell A3, for example, "TEST 01" and "TEST 02" etc.

3. Then, in cell B3 (where we want the test score to appear), enter the following HLOOKUP formula:

=HLOOKUP(A3,Sheet1!1:6,2,0)

Note: In this formula, `Sheet1` refers to the sheet where the data table is located. Your formula may vary depending on where you've created the data table.

After entering the formula, you will see the result:

	A	B	C	D	E
1					
2		STUDENT 02			
3	TEST 01	32			
4	TEST 02				
5	TEST 03				
6	TEST 04				
7	TEST 05				
8					

The formula above is nearly correct but not entirely accurate. This is because if you copy and paste the formula into cells below, you will encounter an error, as shown in the table below:

	A	B	C	D	E
1					
2		STUDENT 02			
3	TEST 01	32			
4	TEST 02	#N/A			
5	TEST 03	#N/A			
6	TEST 04	#N/A			
7	TEST 05	#N/A			
8					

As seen in the table above, the cells below it contains the "#N/A" or "Value not available error." This error occurs because there's an inconsistency in the reference table when the formula is copied to cells below. This is known as "relative calculation," which was discussed in a previous chapter.

The solution is to make the formula more absolute and consistent. To make a formula absolute, you can add a "$" sign before the column or row name that you want to make absolute.

For example, the initial formula:

```
```
=HLOOKUP(A3,Sheet1!1:6, 2, FALSE)
```
```

Can be made absolute like this:

```
```
=HLOOKUP(A3,Sheet1!$1:$6, 2, FALSE)
```
```

To make a formula absolute and add the "$" sign to the formula syntax, you can manually add it, or alternatively, select or highlight the formula starting from "Sheet2!1:6," then press the F4 key on your keyboard until the formula appears as shown.

After you make the formula absolute and consistent, you can see the result in cell B3. At first glance, there may be no difference between cell B3 using the initial formula and cell B2 using the updated formula. However, to see the difference, copy and paste cell B3 into the cells below, and you will get results as shown in the image below:

▲	A	B	C	D	E
1					
2		STUDENT 02			
3	TEST 01	32			
4	TEST 02	79			
5	TEST 03	19			
6	TEST 04	85			
7	TEST 05	86			
8					

From this, it can be concluded that HLOOKUP has the following structure:

The HLOOKUP function is used to perform a search for a value in a horizontal row within a spreadsheet and return the corresponding value from the same row in a different column. Here's the formula structure for the HLOOKUP function:

=HLOOKUP(lookup_value, table_array, row_index_num, [range_lookup])

The components are as follows:

1. `lookup_value`: This is the value you want to search for in the first row (row index 1) of the `table_array`.

2. `table_array`: This is the data range containing the values you want to search for and the values you want to return. This range must include the first row with the search values and the row(s) below it with the values to return.

3. `row_index_num`: This is the row number within

the data range that will be used to return the value. If you want to return a value from the second row within `table_array`, use 2 as the `row_index_num`.

4. `[range_lookup]` (optional): This parameter determines whether the search should be for an exact match (FALSE) or an approximate match (TRUE). Use FALSE for an exact match. If you omit this parameter, Excel will assume it as TRUE by default, which means it will search for the nearest match.

XLOOKUP

XLOOKUP is the latest update to the LOOKUP function, but it has limited compatibility. You can use the XLOOKUP function to solve various table or range-related problems based on rows or columns. With XLOOKUP, you don't need to worry about whether the reference table is arranged vertically or horizontally. XLOOKUP can be used with both types of tables.

For example, if you want to find the price of an automotive component based on its part number or find an employee's name based on their employee ID, XLOOKUP allows you to search in a single column for the search term and return results from the same row in a different column, regardless of which side of the table the returned column is on.

Note: XLOOKUP is not available in Excel 2016 and Excel 2019, and older spreadsheet applications. For full support, it's recommended to use Microsoft Excel online, Google Sheets, or update your spreadsheet application to a more recent version that supports XLOOKUP. However, you may encounter situations where a document created with XLOOKUP in a newer version is opened in an older spreadsheet application (e.g., Excel 2016 or Excel 2019). In such cases, the XLOOKUP function might work fine, but there's no guarantee that it will continue to function correctly when editing the document.

Now, let's try another case study to understand how to use the XLOOKUP function.

Let's recreate the table as discussed in the previous VLOOKUP section:

	A	B	C	D	E
1	Point >=	Predicate	Grade		
2	90	Very well	A		
3	80	Good	B		
4	70	Enough	C		
5	60	Not enough	D		
6	0	Bad	E		

We'll call the table above the "criteria table."

Unlike VLOOKUP; XLOOKUP doesn't require the data in the first column to be sorted from smallest to largest. Sorting is optional. This is one of the advantages of XLOOKUP compared to LOOKUP or VLOOKUP.

Next, let's recreate the main table or simply clear the main table used in the previous exercise, so it looks like this:

	A	B	C	D	E	F
1	NO.	NAME	POINT	PREDICATE	GRADE	
2	1	JOHN	51			
3	2	SMITH	83			
4	3	FATIMA	77			
5	4	ALI	56			
6	5	OMAR	93			
7						

From the previous table, which was worked on using multiple IF statements, we will now attempt to solve it using XLOOKUP.

To complete the PREDICATE, enter the following formula in cell D2:

`=XLOOKUP(C2,Sheet1!A:A,Sheet1!B:B,,-1)`

Compare this formula to the formula you would need to enter if using the VLOOKUP function:

`=VLOOKUP(C2,Sheet1!A:C,2,1)`

Compare this formula to the formula you would need to enter if using the IF function:

`=IF(C2>=90, "Very well", IF(C2>=80, "Good", IF(C2>=70, "Enough", IF(C2>=60, "Not enough", "Bad"))))`

Note: Sheet1 is the name of the sheet where the criteria table is located; the appearance may vary depending on where you create the criteria table.

The XLOOKUP function may look longer than the VLOOKUP function, but it offers flexibility. You don't need to worry about the table's shape (whether it's horizontal or vertical), and you don't need to concern yourself with the data's order (whether it's sorted from smallest to largest or the reverse). XLOOKUP can handle these constraints.

Do the same for cell E2; enter the following formula:

`=XLOOKUP(C2,Sheet1!A:A,Sheet1!C:C,,-1)`

For the cells below, there's no need to type the formula one by one; simply copy the formula from the cell above and paste it into the cells below.

This will result in values as shown in the table below:

	A	B	C	D	E
1	No.	NAME	POINT	PREDICATE	GRADE
2	1	JOHN	51	Bad	E
3	2	SMITH	83	Good	B
4	3	FATIMA	77	Enough	C
5	4	ALI	56	Bad	E
6	5	OMAR	93	Very well	A

In summary, the XLOOKUP function is a powerful lookup function that allows you to search for values within a specific range and return corresponding values from another range. The general structure of the XLOOKUP formula is as follows:

`=XLOOKUP(lookup_value,        lookup_array, return_array,        [if_not_found],        [match_mode], [search_mode])`

Here's an explanation of each part of the XLOOKUP formula:

1. `lookup_value`: This is the value you want to find in the `lookup_array`. It's the value that serves as the basis for the lookup.

2. `lookup_array`: The range of data containing the values you want to search for. The XLOOKUP function will search for the `lookup_value` within the `lookup_array`.

3. `return_array`: The range of data containing the values to be returned if the lookup is successful. The result will be taken from the `return_array` corresponding to the position of the matching value in the `lookup_array`.

4. `[if_not_found]` (optional): This parameter allows you to specify a value to be returned if there is no match in the `lookup_array`. It's an optional value.

5. `[match_mode]` (optional): This parameter determines the matching mode. There are several options like "0" (exact match), "1" (closest match less than or equal to `lookup_value`), "-1" (closest match greater than or equal to `lookup_value`), and others. This is optional, and if not specified, it defaults to "0" (exact match).

6. `[search_mode]` (optional): This parameter determines whether the search is done from the start to the end or the reverse. You can use "1" (search from start to end) or "-1" (search from end to start). This is optional, and if not specified, it defaults to "1" (search from start to end).

11 LOGICAL AND/OR

In spreadsheet applications, especially Microsoft Excel, there are at least four logical functions used to operate on logical values: AND, OR, XOR, and NOT. These functions are extremely useful when you need to perform multiple logic comparisons in a formula or when you want to test multiple conditions at once, not just one. Similar to logical operators, Excel's logical functions return either TRUE or FALSE when their arguments are evaluated.

Here's a brief summary of each of these logical functions to help you choose the right formula for solving specific cases:

1. AND:

The AND function tests multiple conditions and returns TRUE only if all the tested conditions evaluate to TRUE. If any of the conditions is not met or results in FALSE, the function returns FALSE.

Example: =AND(TRUE, TRUE, FALSE) will return FALSE because one of the conditions is FALSE.

2. OR:

The OR function tests multiple conditions and returns TRUE if at least one or more of the tested conditions are TRUE. If all the conditions are false, it returns FALSE.

Example: =OR(TRUE, FALSE, FALSE) will return TRUE because one of the conditions is TRUE.

3. XOR (Exclusive OR):

The XOR (exclusive OR) function tests multiple conditions and returns TRUE if the number of conditions that evaluate to TRUE is odd. In other words, XOR returns TRUE if there are an odd number of different TRUE values.

Example: =XOR(TRUE, FALSE, TRUE) will return TRUE because there are two different TRUE values (an odd number).

4. NOT:

The NOT function negates a logical value. If the argument is TRUE, NOT returns FALSE, and vice versa.

Example: =NOT(TRUE) will return FALSE because it negates the logical TRUE value to FALSE.

Example scenario:

Here's a case example in a spreadsheet application that

can be solved using the AND/OR logical functions.

Let's say we have data from a class test, and we want to determine whether the test participants pass or fail based on two criteria:

1. The math score must be greater than or equal to 70.
2. The English score must be greater than or equal to 80.

We can use the AND function to solve this problem.

Create a table in your spreadsheet application, as shown in the example image below:

	A	B	C	D	E	F
1	No.	NAME	MATH	ENGLISH	AVERAGE	RESULT
2	1	STUDENT 01	76	83		
3	2	STUDENT 02	69	100		
4	3	STUDENT 03	61	78		
5	4	STUDENT 04	60	76		
6	5	STUDENT 05	86	61		

In this case, the formula we can use is the AND function because the criteria require both conditions to be TRUE. Enter this formula in cell F2:

`` `=AND(C2 >= 70, D2 >= 80)` ``

Here, C2 represents the math score, and D2 represents the English score. This formula will return TRUE only if both conditions are met: the math score is greater than or equal to 70 and the English score is greater than or equal to 80.

You can see the results in the table below:

	A	B	C	D	E	F
1	No.	NAME	MATH	ENGLISH	AVERAGE	RESULT
2	1	STUDENT 01	76	83		TRUE
3	2	STUDENT 02	69	100		
4	3	STUDENT 03	61	78		
5	4	STUDENT 04	60	76		
6	5	STUDENT 05	86	61		

For the cells below, you don't need to type the formula one by one; simply copy the formula from cell F2 and paste it into the cells below.

	A	B	C	D	E	F
1	No.	NAME	MATH	ENGLISH	AVERAGE	RESULT
2	1	STUDENT 01	76	83		TRUE
3	2	STUDENT 02	69	100		FALSE
4	3	STUDENT 03	61	78		FALSE
5	4	STUDENT 04	60	76		FALSE
6	5	STUDENT 05	86	61		FALSE

Now, let's modify the conditions in this case. The original conditions were:

1. The math score must be greater than or equal to 70.
2. The English score must be greater than or equal to 80.

Let's add an additional condition:

3. The average score must not be below 70.

Now we have three conditions, and to satisfy all of them, we still use the AND function. But before updating the formula according to the conditions, we need to calculate the average score. To calculate the average, you can use the AVERAGE formula in spreadsheet applications.

So, enter the following formula in cell E2 to calculate the average:

`=AVERAGE(C2:D2)`

The result will look like the table image below:

	A	B	C	D	E	F
1	No.	NAME	MATH	ENGLISH	AVERAGE	RESULT
2	1	STUDENT 01	76	83	79.5	TRUE
3	2	STUDENT 02	69	100		FALSE
4	3	STUDENT 03	61	78		FALSE
5	4	STUDENT 04	60	76		FALSE
6	5	STUDENT 05	86	61		FALSE

For the cells below, you don't need to type the formula one by one; simply copy the formula from cell E2 and paste it into the cells below.

	A	B	C	D	E	F
1	No.	NAME	MATH	ENGLISH	AVERAGE	RESULT
2	1	STUDENT 01	76	83	79.5	TRUE
3	2	STUDENT 02	69	100	84.5	FALSE
4	3	STUDENT 03	61	78	69.5	FALSE
5	4	STUDENT 04	60	76	68	FALSE
6	5	STUDENT 05	86	61	73.5	FALSE

Next, update the formula in cell F2. Instead of:

`=AND(C2 >= 70, D2 >= 80)`

44

Change it to:

`` `=AND(C2 >= 70, D2 >= 80, E2 > 70)` ``

For the cells below, you don't need to type the formula one by one; simply copy the formula from cell F2 and paste it into the cells below.

At first glance, the displayed results don't change, as shown in the following table image:

	A	B	C	D	E	F
1	No.	NAME	MATH	ENGLISH	AVERAGE	RESULT
2	1	STUDENT 01	76	83	79.5	TRUE
3	2	STUDENT 02	69	100	84.5	FALSE
4	3	STUDENT 03	61	78	69.5	FALSE
5	4	STUDENT 04	60	76	68	FALSE
6	5	STUDENT 05	86	61	73.5	FALSE

Combined with IF

As explained in the previous section, the functions AND, OR, XOR, and NOT return and provide TRUE or FALSE values. However, the use of the terms TRUE and FALSE may not be very familiar and flexible, especially among non-technical users, as they can lead to misunderstanding. Therefore, we can change the terms TRUE and FALSE in the example above to "PASS" and "FAIL" or other terms that are more easily understood by the general public or terms needed for other conditions.

To change the terms TRUE and FALSE, we can use the IF logical function, which we will combine with

AND/OR logic.

Let's modify the formula from the previous table. Pay attention to the formula in cell F2:

`=AND(C2 >= 70, D2 >= 80, E2 > 70)`

We can change it to:

`=IF(AND(C2 >= 70, D2 >= 80, E2 > 70), "PASS", "FAIL")`

Press Enter, and the values that were previously TRUE will now change to PASS.

For the cells below, you don't need to type the formula one by one; simply copy the formula from cell F2 and paste it into the cells below.

The results will look like the image below:

	A	B	C	D	E	F
1	No.	NAME	MATH	ENGLISH	AVERAGE	RESULT
2	1	STUDENT 01	76	83	79.5	PASS
3	2	STUDENT 02	70	80	75	PASS
4	3	STUDENT 03	61	78	69.5	FAIL
5	4	STUDENT 04	60	76	68	FAIL
6	5	STUDENT 05	86	61	73.5	FAIL

In this formula, IF evaluates the condition we provided, which is (AND(C2 >= 70, D2 >= 80, E2 > 70)), and if the condition is TRUE—all conditions must be met—it will return and display the value "PASS." If not all conditions are met, or if one condition is not met, it will display the value "FAIL." This formula will yield "PASS" if the value in cell C2 is greater than or equal to 70, the value in cell D2 is greater than or equal to 80, and the value in cell E2 is greater than 70; all values and conditions must be met, otherwise, it will result in "FAIL."

XOR

In this book, I believe it is necessary to have a separate subsection dedicated to XOR because the explanation of XOR above may be insufficient and not detailed enough. Moreover, the definition of XOR itself can be quite ambiguous and confusing.

Therefore, to eliminate and dispel any confusion, let's delve deeper into the XOR function in this discussion.

Let's create a table like the one below:

	A	B	C	D	E	F
1	TRUE	TRUE	TRUE	TRUE	TRUE	
2	FALSE	TRUE	TRUE	TRUE	TRUE	
3	FALSE	FALSE	FALSE	TRUE	TRUE	
4	FALSE	FALSE	FALSE	FALSE	TRUE	
5	FALSE	FALSE	FALSE	FALSE	FALSE	

As discussed earlier, the XOR (exclusive OR) function tests multiple conditions and returns TRUE if the number of conditions that evaluate to TRUE or are true is odd. In other words, XOR returns TRUE if there is an odd number of different TRUE values.

Let's apply XOR to the table above and apply it to the cells highlighted in yellow.

Enter this formula in cell F1:

47

`` `=XOR(A1:E1)` ``

For the cells below, you don't need to type the formula one by one; simply copy the formula from cell F1 and paste it into the cells below.

The results will look like the image below:

	A	B	C	D	E	F
1	TRUE	TRUE	TRUE	TRUE	TRUE	TRUE
2	FALSE	TRUE	TRUE	TRUE	TRUE	FALSE
3	FALSE	FALSE	FALSE	TRUE	TRUE	FALSE
4	FALSE	FALSE	FALSE	FALSE	TRUE	TRUE
5	FALSE	FALSE	FALSE	FALSE	FALSE	FALSE

Remember that XOR will return TRUE if the number of conditions that evaluate to TRUE or are true is odd. Therefore, as seen in the table above, the odd number of TRUE values is in:

Row 1: 5
Row 2: 4
Row 3: 2
Row 4: 1
Row 5: none

So, the rows where the number of conditions that evaluate to TRUE or are true is odd, which are rows 1 and 4, will get a TRUE value; otherwise, it will result in FALSE.

In the real world, XOR may be less commonly used. XOR is more frequently used to solve technical examples. However, you can use XOR to solve cases with two arguments.

48

Suppose you are a human resources professional conducting job applicant selection. Job applicants must meet one of two criteria (but not both). The required criteria for applicants are as follows: Age > 30 or Experienced (but not both). You have data from job applicants summarized in a table, as follows:

	A	B	C	D
1	NAME	AGE	EXPERIENCED	QUALIFIED?
2	PERSON 01	26	YES	
3	PERSON 02	40	NO	
4	PERSON 03	29	YES	
5	PERSON 04	42	YES	
6	PERSON 05	25	YES	

Remember that a participant or applicant must meet one of the criteria, not both. Therefore, the formula suitable for solving this case is XOR—not OR—because if we use OR, all participants may qualify.

The formula we enter in cell D2 is:

`=XOR(B2 > 30, C2 = "YES")`

After entering the formula, the results will be displayed as shown in the table image below:

	A	B	C	D
1	NAME	AGE	EXPERIENCED	QUALIFIED?
2	PERSON 01	26	YES	TRUE
3	PERSON 02	40	NO	
4	PERSON 03	29	YES	
5	PERSON 04	42	YES	
6	PERSON 05	25	YES	

For the cells below, you don't need to type the formula one by one; simply copy the formula from cell D2 and paste it into the cells below.

	A	B	C	D
1	NAME	AGE	EXPERIENCED	QUALIFIED?
2	PERSON 01	26	YES	TRUE
3	PERSON 02	40	NO	TRUE
4	PERSON 03	29	YES	TRUE
5	PERSON 04	42	YES	FALSE
6	PERSON 05	25	YES	TRUE

Here, we can conclude that the participants who meet the qualification criteria are:

1. PERSON 01
2. PERSON 02
3. PERSON 03
4. PERSON 05

However, one participant named PERSON 04 does not meet the qualification criteria because both criteria are met.

In the example above, we cannot use OR because if we

50

use OR, all participants will qualify. It's a matter of choosing the criteria needed so we can choose which formula to use, either OR or XOR.

12 STATISTICS + IF

Formulas Used to Calculate Data Based on Criteria in Excel, there are various functions that allow you to calculate values based on specific criteria. These functions include SUMIF, AVERAGEIF, COUNTIF, and others. Once you understand and master the SUMIF function, learning similar formulas becomes easier.

SUMIF

Let's start by understanding the SUMIF function with a practical case. Imagine you are a sales manager in a company, and you want to analyse the sales of products over the past few months. You have the following sales data:

	A	B	C	D	E	F	G
1	PRODUCT	SALES	MONTH		PRODUCT	TOTAL	AVERAGE
2	ORANGE	1200	JAN		ORANGE		
3	APPLE	800	JAN		APPLE		
4	ORANGE	900	FEB		PEAR		
5	PEAR	1500	FEB				
6	APPLE	700	MAR		MONTH	TOTAL	AVERAGE
7	PEAR	1100	MAR		JAN		
8					FEB		
9					MAR		

There are three tables in the worksheet, with the leftmost table being the main table, and the two tables on the right are statistical tables.

Here's what we can do:

Suppose we want to know the total sales for the product "ORANGE." In this case, the most suitable formula is SUMIF, which we will apply to cell F2.

The formula looks like this:

`=SUMIF($A$2:$A$7, "ORANGE", $B$2:$B$7)`

Note that the formula above contains the word "ORANGE," which means we want to calculate the total data with the criterion "ORANGE." However, using a formula like this is not recommended because it cannot be applied to other cells.

An alternative formula is:

`=SUMIF($A$2:$A$7, E2, $B$2:$B$7)`

Here, E2 is the cell containing the string data with the value "ORANGE."

The result of this formula will yield values as shown in

53

the table below:

E	F	G	H	I
PRODUCT	TOTAL	AVERAGE		
ORANGE	2100			
APPLE				
PEAR				

For the cells below, there's no need to type the formula one by one; simply copy the formula from the previous cell and paste it into the cells below.

Note: If an error occurs, please double-check if the formula you entered is correct. The formula used is the second one, which has been updated. If you use the first formula, you'll need to manually replace "ORANGE" with "APPLE," as you cannot copy-paste it.

E	F	G	H	I	J
PRODUCT	TOTAL	AVERAGE			
ORANGE	2100				
APPLE	1500				
PEAR	2600				

The structure of the SUMIF formula in Excel can be summarized as follows:

`=SUMIF(range, criteria, [sum_range])`

Here is an explanation of each component in the SUMIF formula structure:

1. `range`: This is the range of cells or data where you want to apply the condition or criteria. This formula will check each cell in this range to match

54

the criteria you specify.

2. `criteria`: This is the condition or criteria that each cell in the `range` must meet. The formula will count the number of cells that meet these criteria. Criteria can be text, numbers, or logical expressions.

3. `[sum_range]` (optional): This is the range of cells that contains numbers you want to sum based on the specified criteria. If you want to sum cells from the `range` that meet certain criteria, you can use this argument. If you don't include `sum_range`, the formula will sum cells within the `range` that meet the criteria.

AVERAGEIF

The next question is: What if you want to know the average sales for the product "ORANGE"? In this case, the most suitable formula is AVERAGEIF, which we will apply to cell G2.

Enter the following formula:

`=AVERAGEIF(A:B, E2, B:B)`

Notice that in this AVERAGEIF calculation, we haven't used absolute ranges; we've used ranges that refer to entire columns—e.g., A:A refers to the entire column A from top to bottom. This eliminates the need for absolute ranges, resulting in a neater and shorter formula, which minimizes the chances of errors. However, it's not recommended to create additional tables below the main table or enter data other than the data in the main table in columns A or B, as this would affect the AVERAGEIF calculation.

The result of this formula will yield values as shown in the table below:

E	F	G	H	I	J
PRODUCT	TOTAL	AVERAGE			
ORANGE	2100	1050			
APPLE	1500				
PEAR	2600				

For the cells below, there's no need to type the formula one by one; simply copy the formula from the previous cell and paste it into the cells below.

E	F	G	H	I	J
PRODUCT	TOTAL	AVERAGE			
ORANGE	2100	1050			
APPLE	1500	750			
PEAR	2600	1300			

The structure of the AVERAGEIF formula in Excel can be summarized as follows:

`=AVERAGEIF(range, criteria, [average_range])`

Here is an explanation of each part of the AVERAGEIF formula:

1. `range`: This is the range of cells that will be analysed based on the given criteria. This function looks for values in the `range` that match the `criteria` and then calculates the average of those values.

2. `criteria`: The criteria used to determine which data to average. Only values that meet these criteria will

be used in the average calculation. The criteria can be text, numbers, or expressions that define conditions.

3. `[average_range]` (optional): This is the range of cells used to calculate the average. If not provided, Excel will use the `range` as the range of values to be averaged. In many cases, `[average_range]` is the same as `range`, but in some situations, you may want to calculate the average of one range of values based on criteria applied to another range.

COUNTIF

Next, if you want to know how many times a product was sold, for instance, you want to count how many times the product named "ORANGE" was sold, the appropriate function to solve this is COUNTIF.

Update the statistical table from the previous example as follows:

E	F	G	H	I	J
PRODUCT	TOTAL	AVERAGE	DATA		
ORANGE	2100	1050			
APPLE	1500	750			
PEAR	2600	1300			

We've added a column labelled "DATA" next to AVERAGE. This column is used to count how many times a product has been sold.

The formula used in cell H2 is:

`=COUNTIF(A:B, E2)`

The result of this formula will yield values as shown in the table below:

E	F	G	H	I	J
PRODUCT	TOTAL	AVERAGE	DATA		
ORANGE	2100	1050	2		
APPLE	1500	750			
PEAR	2600	1300			

For the cells below, there's no need to type the formula one by one; simply copy the formula from the previous cell and paste it into the cells below.

E	F	G	H	I	J
PRODUCT	TOTAL	AVERAGE	DATA		
ORANGE	2100	1050	2		
APPLE	1500	750	2		
PEAR	2600	1300	2		

The conclusion from this formula is that the general structure of the COUNTIF formula in Excel is as follows:

`=COUNTIF(range, criteria)`

1. `range`: This is the range of cells or area to be counted based on certain criteria. This is where you want to search for data that meets the criteria.

2. `criteria`: This is the criteria used to determine which data to count within the specified range. The criteria can be text, numbers, or expressions used to filter data within the range.

Exercise

If you observe, in the sample case table discussed earlier, there is one table that we haven't completed. Armed with the knowledge you've gained; you can solve this table independently using SUMIF and AVERAGEIF functions.

Here is the practice table that you need to complete:

	A	B	C	D	E	F	G	H
1	PRODUCT	SALES	MONTH		PRODUCT	TOTAL	AVERAGE	DATA
2	ORANGE	1200	JAN		ORANGE	2100	1050	2
3	APPLE	800	JAN		APPLE	1500	750	2
4	ORANGE	900	FEB		PEAR	2600	1300	2
5	PEAR	1500	FEB					
6	APPLE	700	MAR		MONTH	TOTAL	AVERAGE	
7	PEAR	1100	MAR		JAN			
8					FEB			
9					MAR			

The part that needs to be completed is the section of the table that looks like this:

MONTH	TOTAL	AVERAGE
JAN		
FEB		
MAR		

13 DATABASES + STATISTIC

In Excel, after learning basic statistical functions like SUM and statistical functions with IF conditions like SUMIF, you can move on to advanced database and statistical functions. Some of the advanced statistical functions you can learn include DSUM, DMAX, DMIN, DAVERAGE, DCOUNT, DPRODUCT, DSTDEV, and more. However, we'll focus on some fundamental functions, and you can adapt the knowledge to other functions as needed.

DSUM

Let's explore a case study that can be solved using DSUM. Imagine you are a manager in a company, and you have employee data in the form of a table like the one below:

	A	B	C	D	E
1	NAME	POSITION	AGE	SALARY	
2	EMPLOYEE 01	MANAGER	32	55000	
3	EMPLOYEE 02	ANALIS	28	42000	
4	EMPLOYEE 03	MANAGER	35	60000	
5	EMPLOYEE 04	ANALIS	30	48000	
6	EMPLOYEE 05	STAFF	24	35000	
7					

From the data in this table, you can extract various pieces of information. For example, you may want to know the total salary of managers or the total salary of employees in position X. In this case, you can use DSUM.

Create an additional table to the right. Refer to the following table:

	F	G	H	I	J
1	POSITION	SALARY	AGE		
2					
3					
4					
5					
6	ABOVE IS TABLE OF CRITERIA				

We'll call this table the "Criteria Table." It's intentionally left blank so that we can input criteria data in the next steps.

Create another table to the right as shown below:

	I	J	K
1		TOTAL SALARY	
2			
3			
4			

Technically, you can place the calculation for the total salary anywhere you prefer. To find the total salary for the "Manager" position, use the DSUM formula in cell J2.

Enter the following formula:

`=DSUM(A:D, "Salary", F1:H4)`

The result of this formula will yield a value as shown in the table below:

	I	J	K
		TOTAL SALARY	
		240000	

This formula calculates the total salary from the entire table because we haven't added the desired criteria to the Criteria Table yet.

To calculate the total salary for the "MANAGER" position, add "MANAGER" as a keyword to the Criteria Table, as shown below:

	E	F	G	H	I
1		POSITION	SALARY	AGE	
2		MANAGER			
3		X			
4		X			
5					
6		ABOVE IS TABLE OF CRITERIA			

Enter "MANAGER" in cell F2 and "X" in cells F3 and F4.

Note: You can replace "X" with any other character; it doesn't need to be empty.

Now, cell J2 will change its value from 240,000 to 115,000. The 115,000 represents the total salary for the "Manager" position (55,000 + 60,000).

I	J	K
	TOTAL SALARY	
	115000	

Change the criteria from "MANAGER" to "STAFF" as shown below:

F	G	H	I	J
POSITION	SALARY	AGE		TOTAL SALARY
STAFF				35000
X				
X				
ABOVE IS TABLE OF CRITERIA				

Now, the total salary corresponds to the "STAFF"

63

position.

What if you want to calculate the total salary for both "MANAGER" and "STAFF" positions? You can add additional criteria below, replacing "X" with additional criteria.

F	G	H	I	J
POSITION	SALARY	AGE		TOTAL SALARY
STAFF				150000
MANAGER				
x				
ABOVE IS TABLE OF CRITERIA				

Now, the total salary corresponds to both "STAFF" and "MANAGER" positions, resulting in 150,000 (35,000 + 115,000).

Now, let's change the criteria to calculate the total salary based on age. Modify the Criteria Table as follows:

E	F	G	H	I
	POSITION	SALARY	AGE	
			<=25	
			x	
			x	
	ABOVE IS TABLE OF CRITERIA			

This table provides new criteria based on age. It calculates the total salary for employees in any position but with an age of 25 or below.

The total salary for employees aged 25 or below are as

follows:

I	J	K
	TOTAL SALARY	
	35000	

Now, let's combine criteria. Suppose you want to calculate the total salary for employees in the "ANALYST" and "STAFF" positions with an age of 30 or above.

Update the Criteria Table as follows:

E	F	G	H	I
	POSITION	SALARY	AGE	
	ANALIS		>=30	
	STAFF		X	
	X		X	

ABOVE IS TABLE OF CRITERIA

The result will be as follows:

I	J	K
	TOTAL SALARY	
	48000	

From these examples, we can conclude that the general structure of the DSUM formula in Excel is as follows:

`=DSUM(database, field, criteria)`

Here's an explanation of each part of the DSUM formula structure:

1. `database`: This is the range of cells or area that contains the data you want to sum or analyse. The database is where you will search for data based on specific criteria.

2. `field`: This is the label or column name from the data that you want to sum. You need to specify the column to be summed within the database.

3. `criteria`: This is the range of cells or area where you specify criteria to filter data within the database. You can use criteria to select specific data to be summed.

DCOUNT

Before discussing the structure of DCOUNT, let's revisit the example above:

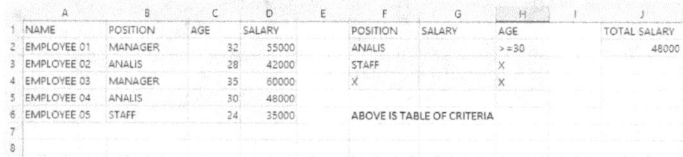

	A	B	C	D	E	F	G	H	I	J
1	NAME	POSITION	AGE	SALARY		POSITION	SALARY	AGE		TOTAL SALARY
2	EMPLOYEE 01	MANAGER	32	55000		ANALIS		>=30		48000
3	EMPLOYEE 02	ANALIS	28	42000		STAFF		X		
4	EMPLOYEE 03	MANAGER	35	60000		X		X		
5	EMPLOYEE 04	ANALIS	30	48000						
6	EMPLOYEE 05	STAFF	24	35000		ABOVE IS TABLE OF CRITERIA				
7										
8										

Update the table on the far right as follows:

I	J	K	L
	TOTAL SALARY	PEOPLE	
	48000		

Suppose you want to count how many employees meet certain criteria. For example, based on the example table above, you know that the total salary for the "STAFF" and "ANALYST" positions with an age of 30 or above is 48,000. Now you want to find out how many employees meet these criteria.

You can solve this using the DCOUNT formula.

Enter the following formula in cell K2:

`=DCOUNT(A:D, "Salary", F1:H4)`

The result of this formula will yield a value as shown in the table below:

I	J	K	L
	TOTAL SALARY	PEOPLE	
	48000	1	

This means there is 1 person who meets these criteria.

Let's modify the criteria table by removing the age

criteria as shown below:

E	F	G	H	I
	POSITION	SALARY	AGE	
	ANALIS			
	STAFF			
	X			
	ABOVE IS TABLE OF CRITERIA			

Now, we'll calculate both the total salary and the number of employees meeting the criteria. In this case, the criteria are based on the "ANALYST" and "STAFF" positions without an age limit.

The result will be as follows:

I	J	K	L
	TOTAL SALARY	PEOPLE	
	125000	3	

The total salary is 125,000, and there are 3 employees who meet these criteria.

From these examples, we can conclude that the general structure of the DCOUNT (Database Count) formula in Excel is as follows:

`=DCOUNT(database, field, criteria)`

Here's an explanation of each part of the DCOUNT

formula:

1. `database`: This is the range of cells or area that contains the database you want to count. The database is a collection of data that includes records or entries you want to filter based on specific criteria.

2. `field`: This is the cell or area that contains the label or column name that corresponds to the numeric data you want to count. In the database, this is the column you want to count.

3. `criteria`: This is the range of cells or area that contains the criteria you want to apply to the database. The criteria should be outside the database and have the same format as the column headers in the database.

DMAX & DMIN

In essence, there isn't a significant difference between DSUM, DCOUNT, and DMAX or DMIN. All of them have similar functions and the same formula structure.

For clarity, let's revisit the previous example:

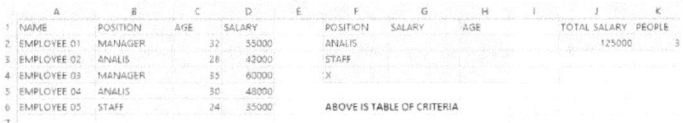

Suppose you want to find the highest and lowest values within a dataset. Based on the previous example, you already have calculated data, such as the total salary and the count of employees meeting certain criteria. Now you want to find the highest and lowest salary amounts among the data that meet these criteria.

Modify the table as shown below:

I	J	K	L	M	N
	TOTAL SALARY	PEOPLE	MAX	MIN	
	125000	3			

To find the highest value and the lowest value, you can use the DMAX and DMIN formulas.

E	F	G	H	I
	POSITION	SALARY	AGE	
	ANALIS			
	STAFF			
	X			
	ABOVE IS TABLE OF CRITERIA			

For the highest value, enter the following formula in cell L2:

`=DMAX(A:D, "Salary", F1:H4)`

The result of this formula will yield a value as shown in the table below:

I	J	K	L	M	N
	TOTAL SALARY	PEOPLE	MAX	MIN	
	125000	3	48000		

To find the lowest value, enter the following formula in cell M2:

`=DMIN(A:D, "Salary",F1:H4)`

The result of this formula will yield a value as shown in the table below:

I	J	K	L	M	N
	TOTAL SALARY	PEOPLE	MAX	MIN	
	125000	3	48000	35000	

From these examples, we can conclude that the general structure of the DMAX (Database Maximum) and DMIN (Database Minimum) formulas in Excel is as follows:

DMAX formula:

`=DMAX(database, field, criteria)`

DMIN formula:

`=DMIN(database, field, criteria)`

Here's an explanation of each part of the DMAX and DMIN formulas:

1. `database`: This is the range of cells or area that contains the database you want to find the maximum (for DMAX) or minimum (for DMIN) value from. The database should include the columns you want to analyse using these functions.

2. `field`: This is the column in the database that you want to find the maximum (for DMAX) or minimum (for DMIN) value from.

3. `criteria` (optional): This is the criteria used to filter the data in the database before finding the maximum or minimum value. You can use criteria to select specific data for analysis. This parameter is optional; if not included, the function will find the maximum or minimum value from the entire database.

DAVERAGE

Similar to AVERAGE, the DAVERAGE formula calculates the average value. However, DAVERAGE requires a criteria table that can be adjusted or modified as needed.

For clarity, let's find the average value in the previous example:

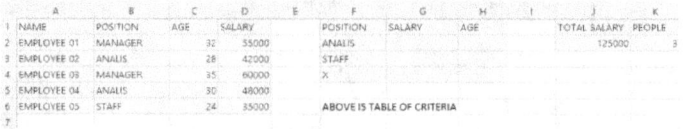

	A	B	C	D	E	F	G	H	I	J	K
1	NAME	POSITION	AGE	SALARY		POSITION	SALARY	AGE		TOTAL SALARY	PEOPLE
2	EMPLOYEE 01	MANAGER	32	35000		ANALIS				125000	3
3	EMPLOYEE 02	ANALIS	28	42000		STAFF					
4	EMPLOYEE 03	MANAGER	35	60000		X					
5	EMPLOYEE 04	ANALIS	30	48000							
6	EMPLOYEE 05	STAFF	24	35000		ABOVE IS TABLE OF CRITERIA					
7											

Add a column labelled "AVERAGE" next to "MAX" as shown below:

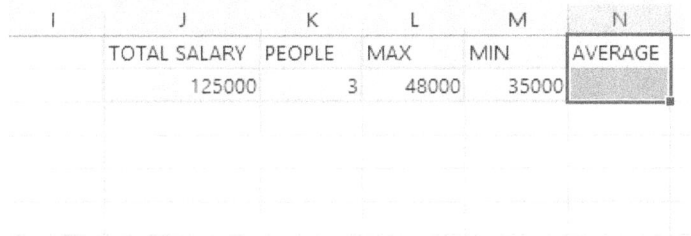

I	J	K	L	M	N
	TOTAL SALARY	PEOPLE	MAX	MIN	AVERAGE
	125000	3	48000	35000	

Using the same criteria as in the Criteria Table:

E	F	G	H	I
	POSITION	SALARY	AGE	
	ANALIS			
	STAFF			
	X			
	ABOVE IS TABLE OF CRITERIA			

Calculate the average value based on these criteria.

Enter the following formula in cell N2:

`=DAVERAGE(A:D, "Salary", F1:H4)`

The result of this formula will yield a value as shown in the table below:

I	J	K	L	M	N
	TOTAL SALARY	PEOPLE	MAX	MIN	AVERAGE
	125000	3	48000	35000	41666.67

From these examples, we can conclude that the general structure of the DAVERAGE formula in Excel is as follows:

`=DAVERAGE(database, field, criteria)`

Here's an explanation of each part of the DAVERAGE formula:

1. `database`: This is the range of cells that contains the database, including column headers. This range encompasses all the data you want to use in the DAVERAGE calculation.

2. `field`: This is the column header within the database that contains the numeric data you want to calculate the average for.

3. `criteria`: This is the range of cells or area containing the criteria you want to apply to the database. The criteria should be placed outside the database and have the same format as the column headers within the database.

Please note that in the DAVERAGE formula, the database should have the first row containing column labels or headers, and subsequent rows should contain data that corresponds to those labels.

14 PRINTING

Printing documents is an essential step in computer operations. This step focuses on converting digital information into a physical format that can be seen, touched, and easily shared. The printing process involves several stages that involve both software and hardware, working together to produce accurate and high-quality copies of digital documents stored on a computer or other devices.

In addition to printing documents in physical form, we also have the option to print in digital formats such as PDF (Portable Document Format) and XPS (XML Paper Specification). This allows us to create electronic copies that can be accessed, shared, and archived more conveniently. Here is a more detailed explanation of printing in PDF and XPS formats:

1. PDF (Portable Document Format): Printing in PDF format creates an electronic copy that preserves the layout, formatting, and visual elements of the original document. PDF is a

format that can be accessed by various devices and operating systems without the need for special software. This makes it suitable for sharing documents with others, especially if we want to ensure that the appearance and formatting remain consistent. Printing to PDF generally involves selecting "Save as PDF" or "Print to PDF" in the print menu of the application we are using.

2. XPS (XML Paper Specification): XPS is a format developed by Microsoft as an alternative to PDF. It serves a similar purpose, which is to produce digital documents with preserved appearance and formatting. XPS format uses XML technology to describe document content. However, the use of XPS is more common within the Windows ecosystem and may require additional software to open on some other operating systems.

Printing in PDF or XPS format has important benefits. First, it allows us to send documents that can be viewed and printed accurately by recipients, without worrying about device or software compatibility. Second, documents in these formats can be digitally archived for future reference, reducing the need to collect physical copies.

In both cases, converting documents into digital formats like PDF or XPS expands our options for sharing and preserving information, whether in physical or digital form, according to individual needs and preferences.

Pre-Printing Preparations

Before printing a document, there are several factors to consider. These are intended to ensure that we can print the file correctly, saving time and resources – for example, avoiding the cost of wasted paper due to incorrect document printing – and more.

Some of the things to consider before printing include:

1. Pay Attention to Paper Size:
   Paper size is a crucial factor to consider before printing a document. Standard papers come in various sizes, such as A4, A3, F4, letter, and legal. Some standard paper sizes can be seen on the paper label or easily measured using a ruler manually.

   Here are some internationally recognized paper sizes:

   1) Letter (North America): This paper size is 8.5 x 11 inches or approximately 216 x 279 mm. It is the most commonly used paper size in North America.
   2) Legal (North America): Legal paper size is 8.5 x 14 inches or approximately 216 x 356 mm. Legal is longer than Letter.
   3) A4 (International): A4 paper size is 210 x 297 mm or approximately 8.27 x 11.69 inches. It is the most commonly used paper size worldwide, except in North America.
   4) A3 (International): A3 paper size is 297 x 420 mm or approximately 11.69 x 16.54 inches. A3 is larger than A4 and is often used for printing pictures, posters, or larger documents.
   5) A5 (International): A5 paper size is 148 x 210 mm or approximately 5.83 x 8.27 inches. A5 is smaller than A4 and is often used for printing books, pamphlets, or postcards.
   6) F4 (Japan & Indonesia): F4 paper size is 210 x 330 mm or approximately 8.27 x 12.99 inches.

It is larger than the more commonly used A4 paper size internationally. F4 paper is primarily used in Japan and Indonesia for printing documents such as business reports, brochures, and similar documents.

2. Consider Orientation:

Generally, spreadsheet applications are used to create tables and data organized in columns and rows.

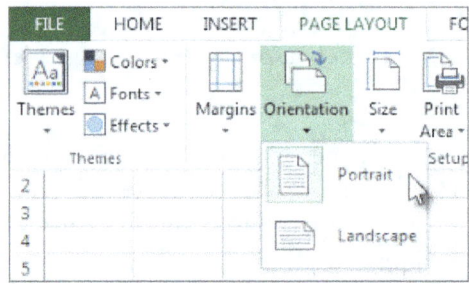

Some tables are vertically oriented, especially those with a lot of data, and in such cases, the most suitable orientation is portrait.

	A	B	C	D	E
1	NAME	POSITION	AGE	SALARY	
2	EMPLOYEE 01	MANAGER	40	2562	
3	EMPLOYEE 02	ANALIS	34	5391	
4	EMPLOYEE 03	MANAGER	35	3008	
5	EMPLOYEE 04	ANALIS	43	7887	
6	EMPLOYEE 05	STAFF	26	7371	
7	EMPLOYEE 06	MANAGER	37	8864	
8	EMPLOYEE 07	ANALIS	48	2481	
9	EMPLOYEE 08	MANAGER	32	1427	
10	EMPLOYEE 09	ANALIS	50	5290	
11	EMPLOYEE 10	STAFF	30	4821	
12	EMPLOYEE 11	MANAGER	41	9807	
13	EMPLOYEE 12	ANALIS	23	8641	
14	EMPLOYEE 13	MANAGER	49	9125	
15	EMPLOYEE 14	ANALIS	43	9660	
16	EMPLOYEE 15	STAFF	30	8461	
17	EMPLOYEE 16	MANAGER	20	4273	
18	EMPLOYEE 17	ANALIS	30	2719	
19	EMPLOYEE 18	MANAGER	49	7279	

Others may have many column headers but relatively few entries, resulting in a wide table, and in these cases, landscape orientation is preferable.

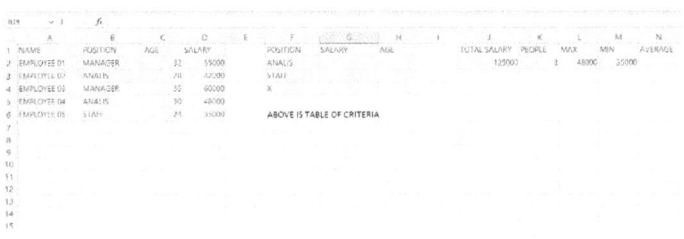

3. Pay Attention to Margins:

Considering margins before printing is an important aspect because the choice of margins significantly affects the printed document's outcome.

There are several common margin settings, such as normal, narrow, wide, and so on, each with different benefits. For example, narrow margins can fit more document content on a single page but may be less aesthetically pleasing and may risk content being cut off or obscured during binding.

On the other hand, wide margins mean less content per page and can be wasteful when printing large volumes of documents.

Therefore, margin settings should be adjusted to fit our needs, or if the document being printed follows specific layout requirements (e.g., for books, theses, or papers), we should adhere to those guidelines.

Here are some reasons why margin settings should be considered before printing:

1) Aesthetics: Balanced and consistent margins make our document look neater and more professional. Documents with overly narrow or inconsistent margins can appear messy or hard to read.
2) Readability: Adequate margins help maintain a distance between text or graphic elements and the paper's edge. This allows readers' eyes to focus more easily on the content and avoids readability issues if text is too close to the edge.
3) Functionality: Margins are also important for keeping essential information in the document from being cut off or hidden during printing. Neglecting margins may lead to the loss of information during printing or unintended cropping on the page.
4) Printing Compatibility: Some printers have physical limitations regarding margins. Printing with extremely narrow margins or exceeding the printer's physical margin limits may result in unexpected outcomes.

5) Design and Format: Margins are part of our document's design and format. Considering margins is an important part of the design process, affecting how our document is received by readers.

6) Official Documents: In some contexts, such as official letters, contracts, or legal documents, there may be specific margin requirements that must be adhered to for the document to remain valid or legally binding.

7) Overall Appearance: Good margins also help organize the overall appearance of our document, including page layout and graphic elements. This can enhance our document's presentation.

8) Measurement Accuracy: Margins are related to measurement and printing accuracy. Ensure that elements in our document (such as tables, graphics, or images) are not cut or distorted due to inadequate margins.

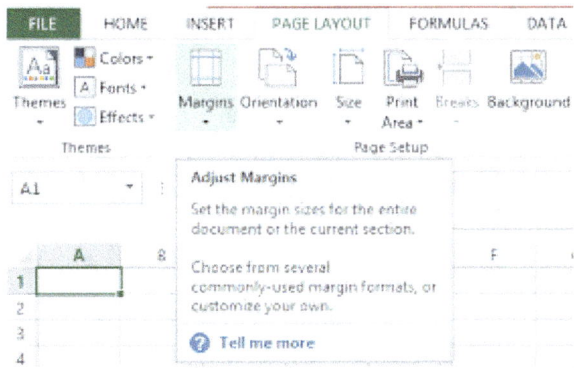

In many cases, word processing, spreadsheet, or specific software programs have margin settings that we can customize according to our needs. It's essential to check these settings before printing to ensure that our document will print correctly and align with our intentions.

4. Consider Repeating Headers:

For tables that are vertically oriented and may be split across multiple pages when printed, consider repeating headers at the top of each page.

This feature ensures that the header row, which typically contains column labels or titles, remains visible at the top of each page, making the table more accessible and easier to understand.

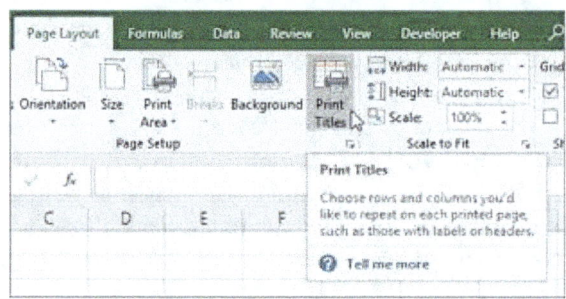

5. Pay attention to the scale

Sometimes, tables created are too wide to be printed, whether in portrait or landscape orientation.

This issue can be addressed by adjusting the document printing scale before the printing process is carried out.

An excessively large table will result in an undesirable fragmented table, and an incomplete table will, of course, render it less informative.

Small fragments of the table may potentially be lost or become concealed, resulting in a flawed table.

Conversely, a table that is too small will appear unattractive – as if the table is wedged among the expanse of the paper – making it disproportionate to the paper's width.

Therefore, it is essential to adjust the scale so that the table to be printed fits perfectly onto the printing medium.

To adjust the scale, you can access it in the layout menu on the ribbon bar.

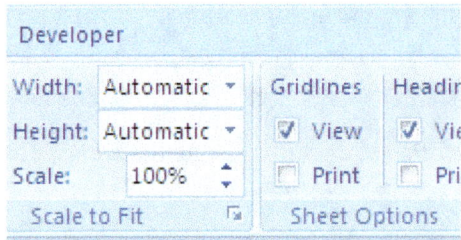

By default, the scale is set at 100%. However, it can be customized, increased, for instance, to 150% if the document to be printed is too small. Consequently, the printed document will have an increased scale.

It can be reduced to 70% if the document to be printed does not fit on one sheet of paper, thereby reducing and adjusting the content according to the scale.

Set Print Area

Print Area in Microsoft Excel or similar spreadsheet applications is a feature that allows document creators to specify which parts or specific areas of their worksheet will be printed or excluded when performing the printing process.

In other words, with print area settings, you can limit

which parts of the worksheet will be printed, rather than printing the entire sheet.

This process can be useful when you only want to print a portion of the data that is relevant in your worksheet.

Here are the steps to define a Print Area in Excel (the printing setup process in other applications may vary):

1. Select the Area to Print:

   a. Open the Excel worksheet you want to print.
   b. Highlight the cells you want to print. You can do this by selecting the cells you want to print. (See the image below)

2. Open the "Page Layout" Tab: At the top of Excel, click on the "Page Layout" tab.

3. Locate the "Page Setup" Group: In the "Page Setup" group, you will find several options related to printing.

4. Click "Print Area": Within the "Page Setup" group, click the "Print Area" option.

5. Choose "Set Print Area": After clicking "Print Area," select the "Set Print Area" option from the menu that appears. This will restrict the selected area as the print area.

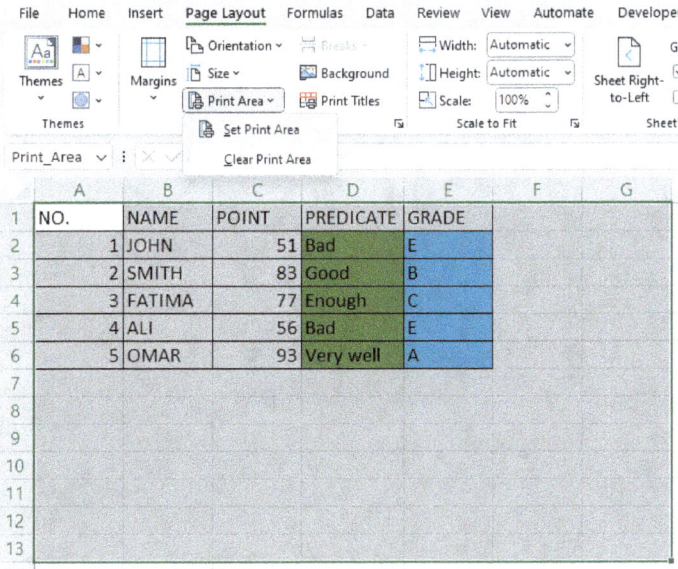

6. Configure or View the Selected Print Area: Now, if you want to check the area you have set as the Print Area, you can click the "Print Area" option again and choose "View Print Area." This process will display the area to be printed with dashed or thin lines. (See the image below)

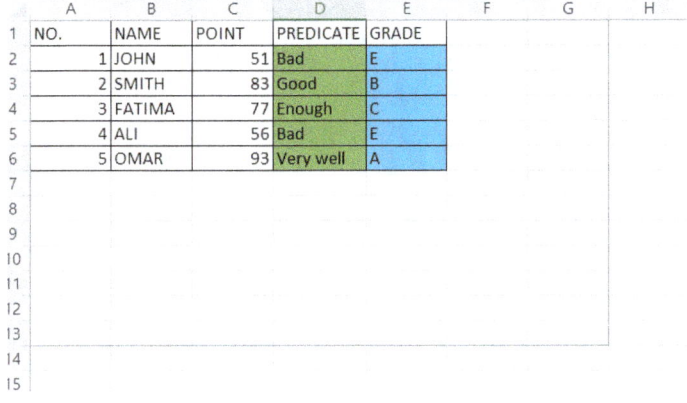

7. Print the Document: Once you've defined the Print Area, you can print the document as usual by using Ctrl+P or going to File > Print. Only the area you specified as the Print Area will be printed. (See the image below)

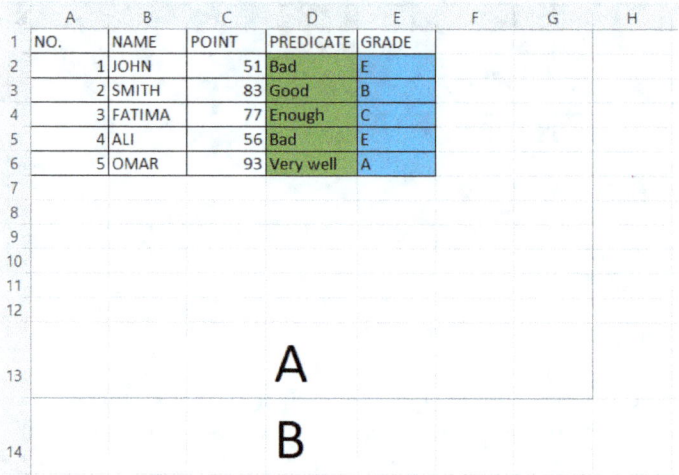

Note: In the images provided, there are letters A and B. Letter A is within the print area, while letter B is outside the print area.

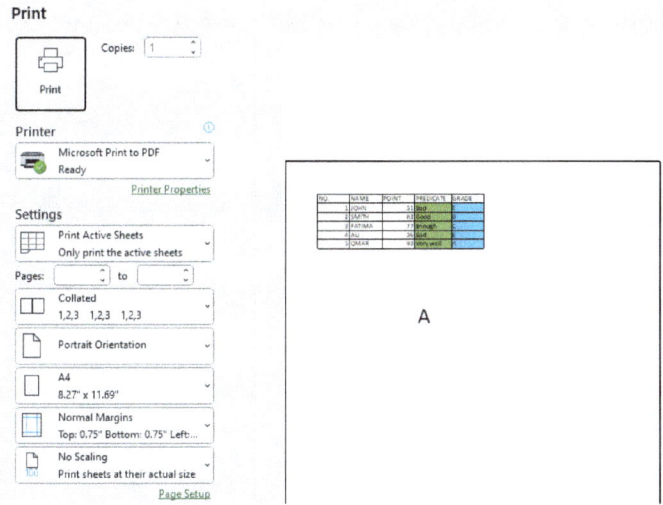

Note: During the printing process, only the content within the print area will be printed – in this case, only letter A, while letter B outside the print area will not be printed.

8. Clearing the Print Area (Optional): If you want to clear the Print Area you have set, you can go back to the "Print Area" option and select "Clear Print Area." (see the image below)

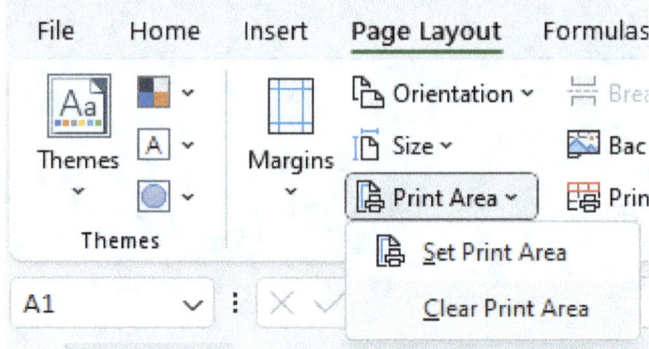

When the print area is cleared, the printing settings will revert to the default, and the printing process will include all content in the worksheet. (see the image below)

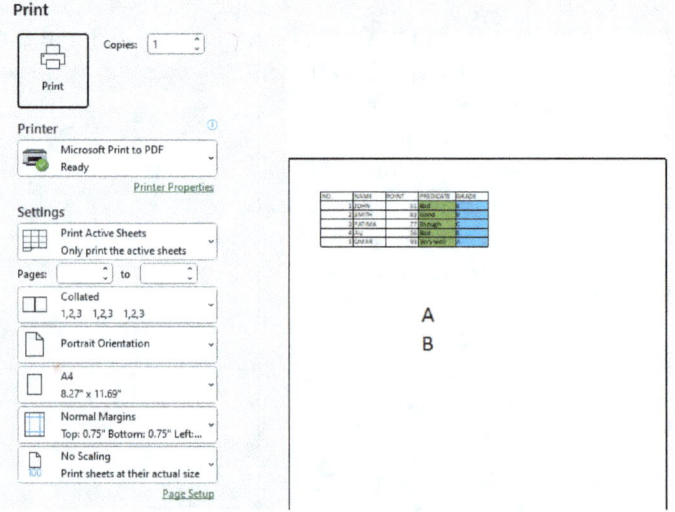

Printing in physical form

Before printing a document, there are several things to consider ensuring a good and efficient print result, including specific printing instructions for spreadsheet worksheets, which can be found in the pre-printing preparation section. Here are some points to consider before printing a document:

1. Choose the Right Printer: Select a printer that is appropriate for the type of document you want to print. Inkjet printers are usually good for printing images and colour documents, while laser printers are more suitable for text and black-and-white documents.

    For worksheets that will be printed in black and white or grayscale, pay attention to colour combinations. Faint colours may print as the same shade, such as yellow and grey printing as grey. Also, ensure that there is enough contrast between text, borders, and fill colours. For example, if the fill colour is dark or intense, make sure the text is in a lighter or brighter colour to ensure readability when printed in black and white.

2. Choose the Right Paper: Select the type of paper that matches the type of document you are printing. Regular paper is suitable for text documents, while photo paper is better for images and photos.

3. Choose the Right Print Settings: In printing applications such as Microsoft Word or Adobe Reader, make sure that the print settings are configured correctly. This includes paper size, orientation, paper type, and print quality, as discussed in the previous sections.

4. Preview the Document: Before printing, use the preview feature available in the application to view how the document will appear when printed. This helps ensure that the layout, text, and other elements are as desired.

5. Print Only What's Needed: Before printing the entire document, consider printing only the pages or sections that are necessary. This can save ink or toner and paper.

    Here's further explanation regarding how to print only the necessary parts in a spreadsheet application, particularly in Excel:

1) Print Only the Active Worksheet:
    Printing the active worksheet is the default option in most applications, including spreadsheets. Generally, there are no specific settings or requirements for printing the active worksheet. The entire document will be printed during the printing process.

    Use the Ctrl+P keyboard shortcut or the print menu to print the entire active worksheet. Make sure to select the "print active sheets" option in the settings.

2) Print the Entire Workbook:

Printing the entire workbook means printing all the content in the spreadsheet file you've created. This option will print all content except for hidden worksheets.

To print the entire document, make sure to select "print entire workbook" in the print options. (see the image below)

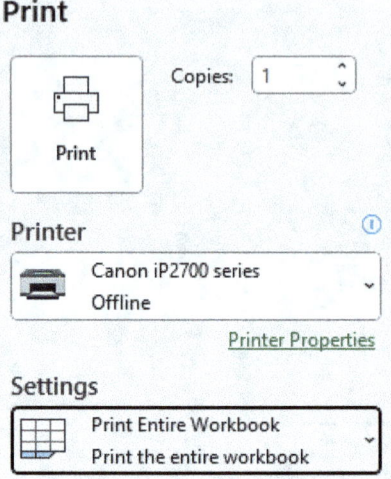

3) Print Only the Print Area:

　　As discussed in a previous section, you can define and specify which area should be printed and which area should not be printed.

　　To set the print area, select the area you want to designate as the print area, then choose "set print area" from the layout menu. (see the image below)

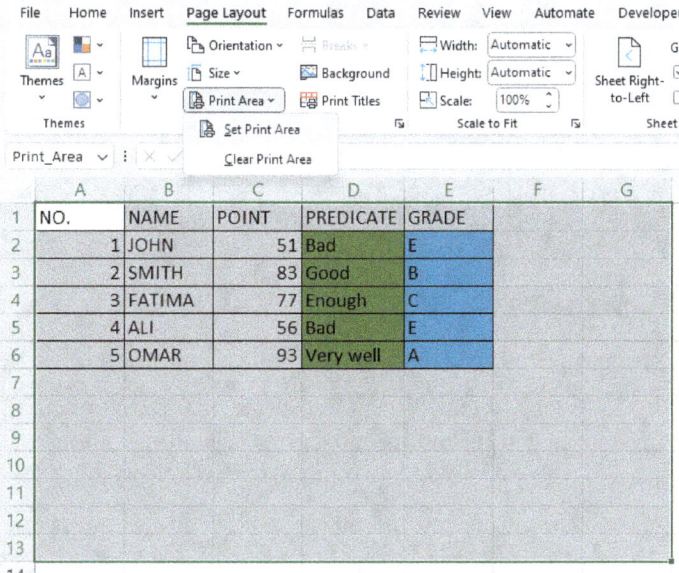

Once the print area is set, you can proceed with printing by pressing Ctrl+P and selecting "active sheets" in the settings.

4) Print Only the Selection:

You can choose to print only specific portions of the worksheet. For example, if you want to print only the first and second columns, select and block the columns you want to print. See the image below:

	A	B	
1	NO.	NAME	POI
2	1	JOHN	
3	2	SMITH	
4	3	FATIMA	
5	4	ALI	
6	5	OMAR	
7			
8			

Next, open the print menu by pressing Ctrl+P and select "print selection." The result will be as shown in the image below:

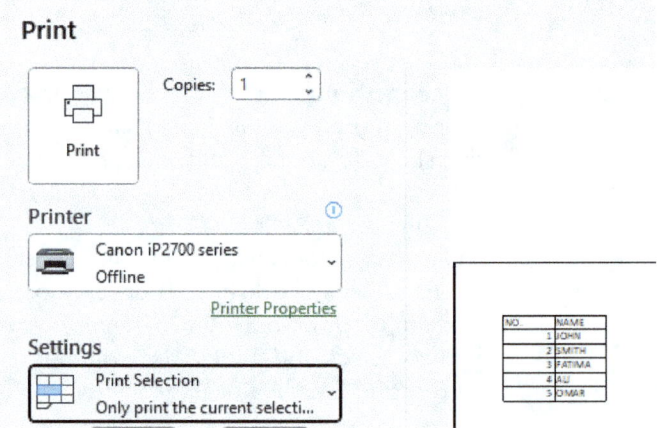

These steps represent common considerations when preparing to print a document. Additional steps may be required if you need further customization and custom printing:

1. Colour Settings: If you intend to print color documents, ensure that the color settings in the

application match your preferences. Determine whether the document should be in full color or black and white.

2. Print Quality Settings: If your printer allows for print quality adjustments, consider these settings. High-quality printing may be better for images and presentations, while normal or draft quality can be used for internal documents.

3. Double-Check Document Content: Ensure that the document has been proofread and edited before printing. This includes checking for spelling, grammar, and overall content accuracy.

4. Save a Digital Copy: After printing the document, consider saving a digital copy as an archive. This can be helpful in case you need additional prints or need to reference the document in the future.

By considering these points before printing a document, you can ensure that the print result meets your expectations and avoid wasting resources such as ink, paper, and time.

Printing in digital format

Sometimes, documents need to be printed in a different format, such as PDF or XPS. Printing in PDF format has many benefits, primarily because PDF preserves the appearance and format of the original document regardless of the device or operating system used. PDFs are also easy to share without worrying about compatibility issues, can be accessed on various platforms, and can be encrypted for security.

PDF documents can be archived effectively, can contain interactive links, and their file size can be compressed. With widely available PDF readers, PDF is the ideal choice for sharing information that needs to maintain its appearance across different devices and environments.

The process of digital printing doesn't significantly differ from physical printing; the main difference lies in the printing medium. Physical printing involves a physical device, such as a printer, while digital printing involves digital software that converts the original format, such as a worksheet, into PDF or XPS.

In broad strokes, the digital printing process follows the same steps as discussed in the "Printing in physical form" section. The only difference is in selecting the digital printing option available on your computer.

Here are the steps:

1. Press the Ctrl+P keys.
2. Choose the "Microsoft Print to PDF" option or another digital printer option that supports digital printing.

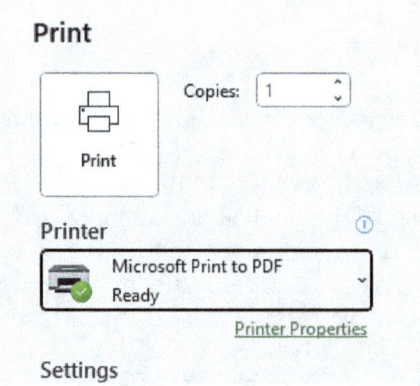

3.   Save the file in the desired directory.

If the above options are not available, for example, if there is no digital printer installed, you can use an alternative method to print in digital format:

Here are the steps:

1.   Open the worksheet you want to print in digital format.
2.   Press F12 or select the "Save As" menu.

3.   In the "Save as type" option, choose "PDF."

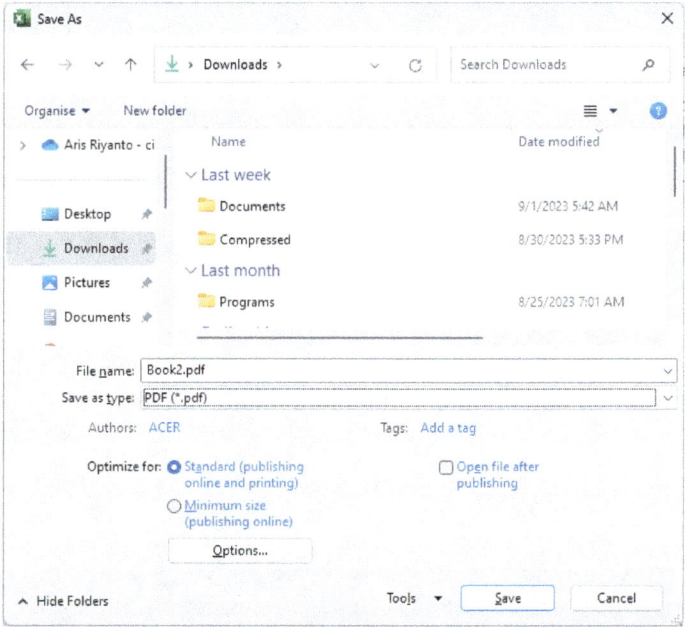

4.   If you want to print in XPS format, select the "XPS document" option and then save.

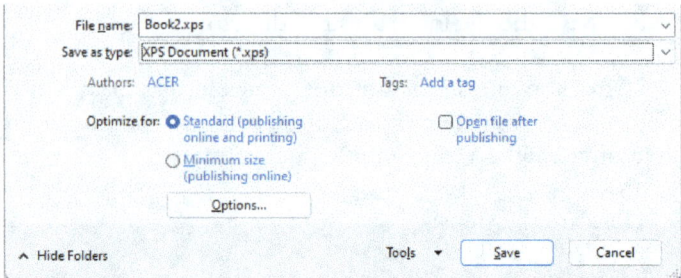

These steps allow you to convert your document into a digital format like PDF or XPS, preserving its content and layout while making it easy to share and archive digitally.

15 EXCERCISE

After reviewing various materials presented in the previous chapters, it's a good idea to sharpen and test our skills in understanding spreadsheet applications, especially Microsoft Excel.

Let's work on the following exercise:

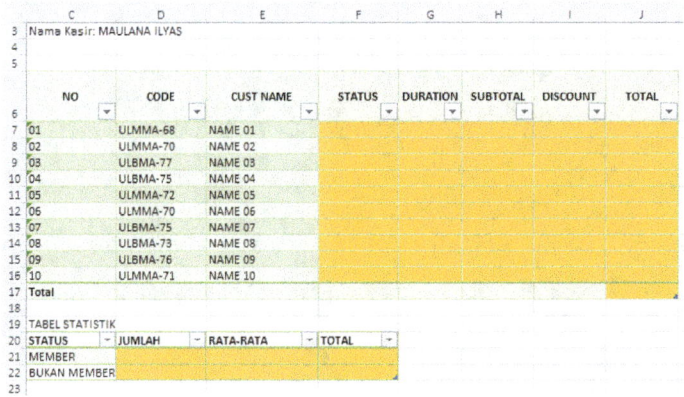

Create a table exactly like the two tables above.

Complete and fill in the empty columns according to the following guidelines:

1. Fill the STATUS column with M or B, based on the character in the middle of the CODE between UL...MA-XX. Or you can fill it with MEMBER and NON-MEMBER.

2. Fill the DURATION column with the code after the hyphen.

3. SUBTOTAL is calculated as DURATION multiplied by 7,500.00 (SEVEN THOUSAND FIVE HUNDRED).

4. DISCOUNT is calculated as SUBTOTAL multiplied by the discount rate.
   a. If it's a MEMBER, they will receive a 50 percent discount.
   b. Otherwise, there is no discount.

ABOUT THE AUTHOR

Aris Riyanto is an Indonesian lecturer who actively teaches at Politeknik LP3I, has a Microsoft Office Specialist (MOS) certification in the field of Microsoft Excel, so he is very competent to write Microsoft Excel for Beginner books.

BIBLIOGRAPHY

Alexander, Michael, Richard Kusleika, and John Walkenbach. *Excel 2019 bible*. John Wiley & Sons, 2018.

Bluttman, Ken. Excel formulas and functions for dummies. John Wiley & Sons, 2013.

Frye, Curtis. Microsoft Excel 2019 step by step. Microsoft Press, 2018.

Alexander, Michael, and Dick Kusleika. Excel 2019 power programming with VBA. John Wiley & Sons, 2019.

Goldmeier, Jordan. Advanced Excel Essentials. Apress, 2014..